ROOM FOR EIGHTY

ERIC REESE

Copyright © 2018 by Eric Reese

All rights reserved.

No part of this book may be reproduced in any form or by any electronic or mechanical means, including information storage and retrieval systems, without written permission from the author, except for the use of brief quotations in a book review.

ISBN: 978-1-925988-35-2

INSPIRATION TO KEEP WRITNG

Dear Eric, thanks for writing. Receiving emails from everyday Americans across our country was one of the best parts of my job as President, and I continue to be touched by stories like yours.

In the extraordinary diversity of opinions and experiences that make up our national character, we see the common sense of purpose and inherent goodness that have always defined who we are as Americans. I appreciate your writing, and I wish you and your loved ones the very best.

— **SINCERELY, BARACK OBAMA**

CONTENTS

The Fastest Rapper Ever!	1
A Real Young Thug	2
The most sincere advice	3
True Superheroes	4
Decades of racism ended	5
Racism in the future?	6
Deep	7
What's deeper!	8
Blacks and Chicanos	9
All is calm on the frontline	10
What's with that?	11
Call me Presidente!	12
No Colors behind the Game	13
Colorless	14
The better decision	15
How about that?	16
Still in Wakanda?	17
Why it got to be us?	18
I'm not the one	19
Dem girls love me	20
A Rapper's Element	21
Tongue-tied	22
The best upbringing	23
Why?	24
Makes you think!	25
Get on down	26
The Realest MC	27
Teacher needs to be taught	28
Dumb ass	29

I can't relate	30
That's bad, Yo!	31
The ultimate stereotype	32
Look at yourself	33
Coincidence	34
We all misjudge	35
Hood Legacy	36
The Weakest Stick-up Ever!	37
Don't try to change	38
The Mind Sprays	39
Living outside the hood	40
Let Daddy and Mommy do them	41
I got those bars, not behind them	42
When being Black is allegedly wrong	43
Nana	44
Breaking racism from within	45
Bond built for decades	46
Help no matter what!	47
Listen up!	48
The Real Heroes	49
Just Hangin' Out	50
Biracial Blues	51
Nature's Blessing in Disguise	52
Don't tell me nothing!	53
From Rags to Riches	54
Street Knowledge	55
Call me Daddy	56
Unmatched	57
The Best Mom Ever!	58
Forgiveness not Forgetting	59
All in Together	60
The Harsh Reality	61
A King for Real	62
He got game	63

A Soldier	64
All in the Same Gang	65
Fight the Power	66
No Casualties of War	67
Real Rap	68
The Obvious	69
Skin Differences	70
I'm Ignorant	71
He's Not	72
So True!	73
Don't mess with the Chicken	74
Black is Black	75
If you didn't know...	76
Mankind's ongoing beef	77
The Experiment	78
Get rid of the Hate	79
This is for you, Mom	80
Acknowledgments	81

THE FASTEST RAPPER EVER!

Bobby won a rap battle in his
    school
saying around ten words a
    second
(maybe a new world record)
... but no one recorded it.

A REAL YOUNG THUG

A young thug while robbing an
    old man
dropped the man's wallet,
and once he saw such beautiful
    memories,
he befriended the elder
and became as him:
a poet.

THE MOST SINCERE ADVICE

"Boy, you came to an uneasy world,
but that only makes victory tastes sweeter."

TRUE SUPERHEROES

One of the kids in my class
said "Hulk!"
and other said "The Flash!"
but it wasn't until
the "Black Panther's" kid came
that the fight stopped.
I said "Classy."

DECADES OF RACISM ENDED

I asked my young son where
    to eat,
he said "K.F.C."
I replied, "Don't you know
    who Sanders is?"
and he said "Dad, it's just
    chicken".
Decades of racism ended by a
    5-year-old.

RACISM IN THE FUTURE?

The year is 3056 and
an old guy still says,
"I'm not racist, but
those aliens disgust me".
Oh, the irony.

DEEP

They say black is the worst of
 colors,
but if you combine all,
what do you get?

WHAT'S DEEPER!

Three African Americans
	sitting
next to the other in court
all with different presents:
a thief, a cop and a lawyer.

BLACKS AND CHICANOS

Those Latino and Black
gangs had been fighting
against one another for
    decades,
not knowing that the problem
    started
from their grandpas, discussing
who would be the first to move
in chess.

ALL IS CALM ON THE FRONTLINE

The streets became
peaceful
when its young folk
decided
to break all barriers.

WHAT'S WITH THAT?

The richest man
in the world
still keeps
his old
shoe polish box.

CALL ME PRESIDENTE!

They mocked me
in class,
calling me Negro, poor,
    colored.

Guess what!
WHO'S YOUR
    PRESIDENT NOW?

NO COLORS BEHIND THE GAME

Martin Luther King, Jr.
once was asked
"Who is your favorite
black player?"

He said, "Isn't the question
who's my favorite player?
We're talking
about games, not colors."

COLORLESS

"Kids, if you want
to be large in this life,
you must see everything
in shades of grey."

THE BETTER DECISION

A little coin to kill my thirst...
or for a bottle of water for
 that man?

HOW ABOUT THAT?

"Even black balloons raise to the sky."

STILL IN WAKANDA?

"Bro, you can't take
a superhero
better
than Black Panther."

WHY IT GOT TO BE US?

So, we, Africans were chillin'
and then you invaded telling us
we're your slaves?
I think you are the ones with
    issues.

I'M NOT THE ONE

"If you think you can
you got me,
you'd better run...

Oh, shit, that chump ran."

DEM GIRLS LOVE ME

You think that
all the girls
at school
are attracted to me
just because
I'm redbone,
isn't racist?

A RAPPER'S ELEMENT

I never thought that I could
have a future in the rap game;
they never taught me that
in public school.

TONGUE-TIED

Seriously, I don't know
why homegirl ran away,
I thought she digged rappers.

Bro, you said rapist, not a
    rapper,
use your bars wisely.

THE BEST UPBRINGING

A kid once wrote:
"I always believed that
black people are more loving,
because my parents are black,
and they gave all the love
they could to someone
they adopted of the opposite
    race."

WHY?

What?
You haven't seen a black man
in a police station before?

No, it's just...
that you have gum in your
    mouth.

MAKES YOU THINK!

There was an actor on the set
of *The Birth of a Nation*
that thought, "Man,
this is kinda' racist."

GET ON DOWN

Bro, you just found
the right one–

So murder him, bumbaclot?

–MURDER?!
I thought
you meant DANCEHALL
   KILLA!

THE REALEST MC

One of these
people out here
is the best MC
of the underground...
I think he's the one
drinking water
from that metal cup.

TEACHER NEEDS TO BE TAUGHT

The homework assignment
    was
"Are people bad?"
And more than one kid
answered "No;
the teacher is worse."

DUMB ASS

"Yo' momma is so dumb,
that if she eats a picture,
she puts it in the microwave
 first."

Bro, we have the same momma.

I CAN'T RELATE

"Who's your superpower,
 Bro?"
I'm black and asking me
for a superpower isn't a thing
you'd ask inside an insurance
 company.

THAT'S BAD, YO!

Yo' bars
are so whack,
you would lose
to deaf people!

THE ULTIMATE STEREOTYPE

People would freak out
if they knew "Negro"
is one of the nicest names
you can call a person of color
in Latin America.

LOOK AT YOURSELF

Sometimes,
I see myself
in the mirror
and I don't see
a person of color,
I see a breadwinner.

COINCIDENCE

If my friends
called me nigga
meaning I was their equal...
what do they call Sammy Sosa
 and Little Kim now,
"Michael Jackson and Miss
 Piggy."
At the end of the day,
we're still black and will
 always be.

WE ALL MISJUDGE

I'll kill you!

Oh, it's because I'm—,
right?!
White boy, you're are freakin'
    racist –

No, dumbass,
it is because you misspelled
"Mississippi" on the final
    exam!

HOOD LEGACY

When the "world's most
    gangsta rapper"
saw the demolition of his
    childhood home,
he couldn't avoid shedding a
    tear...
or two.

THE WEAKEST STICK-UP EVER!

This is a stick-up, give up the
 goods!
*No, this is a contra-stick-up,
 give me your gun!*
–No, this is a contra-contra-
 stick-up, give me your...
I don't know... fuck it, take off
 ya skullie!

DON'T TRY TO CHANGE

It's crazy to think
that people's food
doesn't taste good.

If they try to make black milk,
that would be totally gross.

THE MIND SPRAYS

My family came from a gang
that only knew how to shoot.
For me, I prefer spittin' lyrics
to hurt others. It's far more
    damaging.

LIVING OUTSIDE THE HOOD

I knew it was different,
that our skin colors
would cause mockery
in this upscale neighborhood,
but after you try
a darker body of color,
you cannot leave it.

LET DADDY AND MOMMY DO THEM

"Come," I said to my little
   brother
and took him to the other room;
I played some T.I.
while our parents argued
in the kitchen.

I GOT THOSE BARS, NOT BEHIND THEM

In an interview, an imprisoned
 rapper
mentioned: "I have a week
 to go
before I leave this place and
 I've done
some terrible things.
I don't want to do the same
 things
over again. I want something
 new,
something thorough,
so I started writing
and it was *'For the people...Yes,
 yes, y'all.'*
Hip Hop saved me."

WHEN BEING BLACK IS ALLEGEDLY WRONG

One was killed,
another was down
on the pavement,
and the police grabbed me.
The crime? Being black
and asserting my rights.

NANA

My Nana
was the best woman in the
    world;
she taught me that love wasn't
    measured
by social classes or the color of
    skin,
and although we didn't share
    the same blood,
she always was and will
    continue to be
my family.

BREAKING RACISM FROM WITHIN

The great patriarch of the
>family
could not bear that his little girl
was dating a white freckled
>boy.
But after seeing her happy,
hearing her laugh,
catching them share the
>same look
he once shared with his lost
>wife;
he began to care less about the
>color
of skin, more about the color of
>love.

BOND BUILT FOR DECADES

A child approached
a girl who ate alone at lunch,
and asked her why she was
    sitting alone.
"Nobody sits with me because
    I'm black;
better leave
before they start messing with
    you, too."
The boy, as if he had not heard
    her, sat next to her
and offered her his snack.
Decades of friendship
made in just one second.

HELP NO MATTER WHAT!

My grandmother always said:
    "It doesn't matter
the race. Whenever someone
    needs help,
hold their hand as maybe
    tomorrow it will be you."
She never made mistakes
and that's why I've decided to
    become the first
Black officer in my county.

LISTEN UP!

The teen regretted the moment
    he'd fired a gun.
His father told his son to stay
    away from that life,
but as always; these boys never
    listen until it truly matters.

THE REAL HEROES

"They had been heroes
who made our families proud,
they gave their lives for the
    cause and
although many remember
    them as gangstas,
I would continue to remember
    them
as those who fought for our
    rights
to be heard for the first time."

JUST HANGIN' OUT

His friends were making fools
    of themselves,
rappin' to the hits "of his
    people"
and he couldn't help but laugh.

"Sorry guys,
but you have to die and be born
black to understand the
    struggle."

They all smiled that night.

BIRACIAL BLUES

Daddy was black
and Mommy was white.
The kids made fun of me
　　for that
and I didn't understand why.
I asked Mom
why they're teasing me.
She told me,
"Darling, they only envy you
because they don't have the
　　best of both worlds."

NATURE'S BLESSING IN DISGUISE

I always liked animals,
how they love
and do it no matter what.

That's why
I decided to be a veterinarian,
because my furry clients
aren't going to be scared being
    looked after
by a man of color.

DON'T TELL ME NOTHING!

My people were not
emancipated from slavery
 many years ago
for a rude white man
to come and tell me how his
great-granddaddy was good
to my family.

FROM RAGS TO RICHES

The young king had grown up
    in the streets,
hungry, enduring the cold
    winters of Chicago,
only so that at the end of
    the day,
he would become one of
    the best
businessmen in American
    history.

STREET KNOWLEDGE

"The streets are cold: kill or be
  killed.
So don't be like me.
Even if your friends turn their
  backs
and you're alone,
leave that path and look for
  something better,
because you won't want to be
  on this side of the cell."

CALL ME DADDY

All this man's racism came out
when he discovered
his ex-wife's new husband
was handlin' his business
better than him.

UNMATCHED

Death be better
than not resembling
an incredible brunette
with a puffy Afro.
The problem was
it wasn't brown,
but blonde
and straight, and most
importantly: was not
even a woman's.

THE BEST MOM EVER!

My mother took care of me
and five brothers on the worst
 block in the hood.
Then took us out of the ghetto
and with her hard work,
she made us
rise-up, educated
and turned us into respectable
 young men, fathers and
 husbands.

So yes, if she
–without being able to use the
 words–
managed to do it, anyone can.

FORGIVENESS NOT FORGETTING

I held my composure
for the first time ever
and instead of releasing it,
I preferred to forgive
the white man who killed my
    mother and father.
Because the Lord is all-
    Knowing, the Retributer,
I won't be the one
who ultimately judges him.

ALL IN TOGETHER

For a long time, I've envied
    whites,
for it was as if the world
    loved them
more than us,
but after seeing a white
    homeless family living in a
    box on 5th Avenue,
I realized that at the end of
    the day,
we are all in the same gang in
    this shithole
they call 'America'.

THE HARSH REALITY

"See you later, Mom,
and I'm sorry," said my son
before leaving for the day.
With tearing eyes, I saw
    him go.
I knew it was possible that he
    might not make
it back.

A KING FOR REAL

4/4/1968:
The bullet went through his
 throat;
his speech wasn't finished, and
 the body fell lifeless.
A man died, but his vision was
 remembered forever.

HE GOT GAME

He was a ladies' man from the
    hood,
and when asked of his secret,
    he said:
"Take care of the Afro
as you would take care of your
    mother."

A SOLDIER

He looked at himself
one last time in the mirror,
and goodbye to his family,
> determined
to change a generation,
without knowing he'd die
in the process, but
winning all every battle along
> the way.

ALL IN THE SAME GANG

I realized that blacks
and whites are equal
when we cry
for the same deceased
for the same reasons.

FIGHT THE POWER

Governments created walls
and we, with this poetry,
created bridges
for our brothers and sisters.

NO CASUALTIES OF WAR

"We aren't here
to see the colors of the people;
we're here to save them
without caring about their
    complexions.
This is called what they call
    'war'."

REAL RAP

I thought that my raps
would have destroyed the
 differences
between my brothers; not that
 we would live apart
deciding who was the best;
 East or West.
Hip Hop was the answer and
 most never knew it.

THE OBVIOUS

Our palms are the same color,
maybe that's why
it felt better to shake and
    move on.

SKIN DIFFERENCES

Some complain
about skin color,
while others complain
about skin problems.

I'M IGNORANT

I took a trip through the
 Black Sea
thinking that... well, you know
 what?
What a disappointment!

HE'S NOT

Some white guy
praised me
for being a
pretty
long-haired
African American.
I am Native, Yo! Stop the
    bullshit!

SO TRUE!

They say that
the black person always dies
    first
in horror movies.
Hmm.
No black man or woman
would dare go
into an abandoned cabin
at night in real life, FOOL!

DON'T MESS WITH THE CHICKEN

What I like most
about our chicken
is the dark meat...
What did you think
I'd say?

BLACK IS BLACK

Dear,
if you criticize
my people so much,
why do y'all
wear
all black at funerals?

IF YOU DIDN'T KNOW...

Why do some people say
in antiquity that
God created all people equal,
but despise people of color?

MANKIND'S ONGOING BEEF

Do you know what
is regrettable?
That although
racial hatred is despised,
mankind will invent
new excuses
to keep it going.

THE EXPERIMENT

Just imagine
if whites were forced
to live on an island
with a bunch of black people
as a scientific experiment.
What would be the result?
–All of them would eat
crabs and seafood together.
Stupidity breaks all
    boundaries.

GET RID OF THE HATE

I'm sick and tired
of all these racist ass jokes;
why don't we stand together
and stop all the hate...
and kill all spiders!
(Honestly, I hate spiders.)

THIS IS FOR YOU, MOM

My mom always told me
that I would
be great one day,
that I'd
have a nice house, a nice car,
    and a fat bank account
and that's the way
it was supposed to be.

That's why, Mom,
this one's for you. I'm still
    grindin'.

ACKNOWLEDGMENTS

For all the youngsters out there, keep ya heads up and embrace the struggle.

www.ingramcontent.com/pod-product-compliance
Lightning Source LLC
Chambersburg PA
CBHW032359100526
44587CB00010BA/586